BE BEAUTIFUL • BE INTELLIGENT • BE HEALTHY • BE IMMORTAL

BE SUPERIOR

SUPERIOR IRON MAN

INFAMOUS

Writer Tom Taylor

ISSUES #1-3
Artist Yildiray Çinar
Ink Assists Ruy Jose & Juan Vlasco

ISSUE #4
Penciler Yildiray Çinar
Inkers Cory Hamscher (pp. 1-15)
& Tom Palmer (pp. 16-20)

ISSUE #5
Artist Laura Braga

Colorist Guru-eFX
Letterer VC's Clayton Cowles
Cover Art Mike Choi
Assistant Editor Jon Moisan
Editor Mark Paniccia

Iron Man created by Stan Lee, Don Heck, Larry Lieber & Jack Kirby

Collection Editor Jennifer Grünwald **Assistant Editor** Sarah Brunstad
Associate Managing Editor Alex Starbuck **Editor, Special Projects** Mark D. Beazley
Senior Editor, Special Projects Jeff Youngquist **SVP Print, Sales & Marketing** David Gabriel

Editor in Chief Axel Alonso **Chief Creative Officer** Joe Quesada
Publisher Dan Buckley **Executive Producer** Alan Fine

Tony Stark is a technological visionary...a famous, wealthy and unparalleled inventor. With the world's most advanced and powerful suit of armor, Stark has valiantly protected the innocent as an invincible bright knight known as IRON MAN.

But when his mind was altered, a more selfish and devious personality surfaced. Can Tony Stark still be a hero when he thinks he's superior?

1: NIGHTMARE SCENARIO

WHAT HAS GONE BEFORE...

INDUSTRIALIST TONY STARK IS ONE OF THE SMARTEST AND RICHEST MEN ON THE PLANET. WITH HIS HIGH-TECH ARMOR HE PROTECTS EARTH AS THE INVINCIBLE IRON MAN.

DURING A WORLD-THREATENING BATTLE WITH A PSYCHIC-POWERED RED SKULL, IRON MAN AND AN ARMY OF HEROES DEFEATED THE VILLAIN...

BUT THE PSYCHIC FALLOUT CHANGED THE PERSONALITIES OF THOSE ON THE BATTLEFIELD.

WHILE MOST WERE EVENTUALLY RESTORED, A MORE SINISTER TONY STARK EVADED CHANGING BACK...AND HE HAS SOME SPECIAL PLANS FOR THE WORLD HE SWORE TO PROTECT.

IN THAT MOMENT, AS A CITY DOWNLOADED PERFECTION, TONY STARK WAS THEIR *MESSIAH*.

HOWEVER, LIKE SO MANY CONVERTED ZEALOTS, THEY WERE *BLIND* TO THE TRUTH...

YOU SHOULD MENTION THAT TO HIM.

WHY TEEN ABOMINATION?

HE'S BEEN EXPOSED TO A SMALL AMOUNT OF GAMMA RADIATION. HE'S NOWHERE NEAR THE ABOMINATION'S STRENGTH BUT HE'S PRETTY STRONG.

HOW STRONG?

KNG

UHFFF!

TOOM

PRETTY STRONG.

BEFORE I BEAT YOU DOWN AND EMBARRASS YOU IN PUBLIC--

--I WANT TO TALK TO YOU ABOUT NAMES AND THEIR IMPORTANCE.

WELL...THAT'S
DISORIENTATING.

...

TSSSSS.

WHAT
THE HELL?

WHEN YOU SAID YOU'D MEET ME INSIDE, I DIDN'T THINK YOU WERE GOING TO TAKE AN HOUR.

I DIDN'T THINK I'D BE AN HOUR EITHER, BUT SOME OF THE GIRLS OUT THERE HAVE NO REGARD FOR PUNCTUALITY.

YOU'RE DRINKING AGAIN?

I AM. A LOT. I HAVE TO MAKE UP FOR ALL THOSE WASTED YEARS OF SOBRIETY.

NOW, IS THERE SOMETHING I CAN HELP YOU WITH, PEPPER?

OR HAVE YOU COME ALL THE WAY TO SAN FRANCISCO JUST TO GIVE ME *DISAPPROVING LOOKS?*

"--ARE YOU TELLING ME THAT YOU CAN'T SEE WHAT WILL HAPPEN?

"YOU'VE CREATED A MASTER RACE ACROSS THE CITY, BUT YOU'VE ALSO CREATED AN INSTANT UNDERCLASS."

HEY!

"EXTREMIS MAY HAVE MADE PEOPLE MORE BEAUTIFUL ON THE OUTSIDE BUT YOU KNOW AS WELL AS I DO THAT, FOR SOME--"

HEY!

"--IT WILL ONLY ENHANCE ALL OF THE UGLINESS WITHIN."

HEY. I'M TALKING TO YOU!

SOCK

WE DON'T WANT YOU IN OUR CITY.

WHAT DID I DO?

WHAT DID YOU *DO?* STARK MADE US ALL BEAUTIFUL AND YOU STAYED LIKE THAT. ONE HIDEOUS *BLEMISH.*

THNK

HNF!

BACK UP. DON'T MAKE ME--

GHRK!

WHAT DID YOU DO TO ME?

WHAT ARE YOU TALKING ABOUT? I HAVEN'T DONE ANYTHING YET...

NO...

SOMETHING'S WRONG!

SOMETHING'S... NAAAAAGH!

STARK.

"I HEAR WHAT YOU'RE SAYING--"

PLEASE.

WHAT DID YOU DO?

PLEASE... GIVE IT BACK!

TONY, WHAT THE *HELL* DID YOU *DO*?

DEET DEET

WHAT DID I DO? I JUST LAUNCHED THE CORNERSTONE OF THE NEW STARK INDUSTRIES.

I LET THEM ALL FEEL PERFECTION.

EXTREMIS 3.0

FREE TRIAL PERIOD OVER

DAILY RENEWAL

$99.99

--TONY ALWAYS SAID HIS BIGGEST FEAR WASN'T THE WRONG PEOPLE GETTING THEIR HANDS ON HIS TECHNOLOGY, HIS WEAPONS, HIS FRIENDS OR EVEN HIS LOVERS.

WHEN HE TOLD ME WHAT IT WAS, I THOUGHT IT WAS EGO. BUT I UNDERSTAND NOW.

BECAUSE THE NIGHTMARE SCENARIO HAS HAPPENED.

HIS *MIND* HAS BEEN *TAKEN.*

WE NEED TO ACTIVATE THE CONTINGENCY.

UNDERSTOOD.

IT'S OKAY, PEPPER...

200

100

70

50

2: DAREDEVIL VS. IRON MAN

I WON'T HOLD THIS LITTLE OUTBURST AGAINST YOU.

YOU KNOW YOU'RE ALWAYS WELCOME. BUT IF YOU *DO* COME BACK...

...COAT-CHECK THE ATTITUDE.

Right. Well--

--that could have gone better.

SPSSSHHH

I hate the sea. It's one of the places where my radar sense is *useless.*

Amplified sound with no direction. No sense of smell. No touch.

Nature's sensory deprivation tank.

And from the height I've just fallen from, I have no idea how deep I am.

The only way to know which way is up is from the decreasing pressure on my eardrums.

But I'm not thinking about that.

All of my abilities have been replaced by wild thrashing while my brain screams "*Don't drown.*"

HUUURGH!

I can hear the party. I can hear the excitement. The adrenaline. Everything has increased. Tony's guests have been fueled by him throwing me out of there.

Confronting him at home was stupid. Way too public. I just gave him a chance to *show off.*

And Tony Stark has always loved an audience.

LADIES AND GENTLEMEN. THAT WAS OUR ENTERTAINMENT FOR THE EVENING, DAREDEVIL, THE MAN WITHOUT FEAR!

THOUGH I HAVE TO SAY, FOR A *"MAN WITHOUT FEAR,"* AS HE WAS FALLING THROUGH THE AIR, HE LOOKED JUST A TEENSY-BIT WORRIED.

NOW, OUR PARTY-CRASHER WENT ABOUT IT THE WRONG WAY, BUT HE WAS TRYING TO EXPLAIN THAT THERE IS AN ISSUE, AND I'M NOT UNSYMPATHETIC.

THE NEXT DAY. CASTRO STREET...

...TWO AND A HALF HOURS AFTER MIDDAY.

I HAD A PARTY LAST NIGHT THAT EVEN EXTREMIS CAN'T HELP ME FULLY RECOVER FROM.

I SEE YOU WALKING THROUGH THE STREET. I SEE WHAT YOU'VE TURNED THESE PEOPLE INTO. HOW THEY FAWN.

GREAT. YOU'RE VERY PERCEPTIVE.

YOU CAN'T BUY THEM WITH THIS.

THEY DON'T LOVE YOU.

Congratulations on being close to Tony! Enjoy 24 hours of Extremis for free. Just click "Accept".

ACCEPT

I LOVE YOU, TONY!

STARK F.T.W!

THAT GUY LOVES ME.

STARK F.T.W!

A COUPLE OF RULES. I KNOW THIS IS VERY EXCITING BUT I'D APPRECIATE IT IF YOU TRIED NOT TO TRAMPLE THOSE AROUND YOU.

IT'S HARD TO BE A SHINING HUB OF HOPE WHEN PEOPLE ARE SCREAMING.

ALSO-- SCREAMING-- NONE OF THAT.

I KNOW WHAT YOU'RE DOING.

MY SON. HE...I HAVE STRUGGLED WITH ADDICTION ALL MY LIFE. HE HAD ESCAPED MY CURSE, AND THEN YOU--

--YOU TURNED HIM OVERNIGHT. YOU DIDN'T EVEN GIVE HIM A CHOICE.

YOU'RE A MONSTER.

OF COURSE I GAVE HIM A CHOICE. DOES NO ONE READ THE USER AGREEMENT BEFORE THEY CLICK "ACCEPT"?

PLEASE. YOU AND I BOTH KNOW THAT YOU'RE NOT GOING TO--

--IT'S A *VERY* LONG WAY DOWN.

YOU BASTARD.

Congratulations on being close to Tony! Enjoy 24 hours of f... this for f... just click "accept".

DEET

THERE. WAS THAT SO HARD?

HOW DO YOU FEEL?

INCREDIBLE.

DAMN STRAIGHT.

NOW SMILE.

No one else heard their conversation.

But I heard every word--

MATT?

I'm in my bed. I can smell it. But...

COME ON. I DIDN'T HIT YOU THAT HARD.

AND WATCHING YOU SLEEP IS STARTING TO FEEL CREEPY.

But something's wrong.

MATT!

THAT'S IT. RISE AND SHINE.

I SAID I HAD SOMETHING FOR YOU.

My God.

3: MAN OF VISION

I KNOW WHAT YOU'RE THINKING.

YOU'RE A VERY LUCKY MAN, MATT MURDOCK.

YOU GET TO SEE AGAIN.

AND THE FIRST FACE YOU GET TO SEE IS *THIS* ONE.

IT'S ALL SO... CONNECTED.

WE'VE ADVANCED VERY QUICKLY. SOME WOULD SAY TOO QUICKLY. IT'S NOT THE WORLD YOU WERE A PART OF.

NO...

...IT'S STARTED TO CATCH UP.

HE MUST THRIVE HERE.

OF COURSE. TONY'S HAD A HAND IN HALF THE ADVANCES YOU'RE SEEING.

Iron Man, bring #Extremis to New York!

I want me some #Extremis!

I can't afford Extremis anymore. #Hurts.

Anybody hook me up with #Extremis until pay day? Will do ANYTHING.

Food or Extremis? #StarksWorldProblem

HE'S LOST.

HE'S TWISTED.

CAN WE ACT?

NOT YET. THE WORLD HAS CHANGED SO MUCH. I NEED TO DOWNLOAD IT ALL.

BUT WHAT HE'S DOING NOW...

YES. I CAN SEE. THEY'RE ALL TALKING ABOUT HIM.

THE CONTINGENCY WE PREPARED WAS FOR A DIFFERENT AGE, PEPPER.

I NEED TO ADAPT.

THE NEW
STARK ISLAND.
ALCATRAZ.

KAOOOM

AGHHHHH!

STARK!

WHERE
ARE YOU?

OH, MAN! THAT WAS...

THANK YOU!

CAN YOU SWIM?

WHAT?

UM...YEAH? I CAN SWIM. BUT WHY--?

AAAAGHHH!

SPSSSHH

TELL ME WHAT YOU WANT.

WHAT I WANT?

YOU CAME HERE LOOKING FOR ME. YOU BROKE ALL MY STUFF. YOU USED MY MOTORBIKES AS PROJECTILE WEAPONS. YOU CLEARLY WANT SOMETHING.

WHAT IS IT?

I...I TRIED EXTREMIS. IT DIDN'T DO ANYTHING.

I JUST WANT YOUR HELP.

AND *THIS* IS HOW YOU ASK FOR HELP?

YOU'RE A GIANT GREEN BALL OF ANGER AND PUBERTY.

OF COURSE THIS IS HOW YOU ASK FOR HELP.

...YEAH.

YEAH, OKAY. I'LL TALK TO S.H.I.E.L.D.

GET UP AND START CLEANING UP YOUR MESS.

I CAN USE YOU.

4: THE CHOICE

"--IRON SIGHT.

"A NETWORK OF DRONE CAMERAS, DESIGNED TO PROTECT ALL OF YOU, IS SPREADING THROUGHOUT THE CITY AS I SPEAK."

WHEN USERS DOWNLOADED THE FREE EXTREMIS APP, YOUR DATA WAS UPLOADED TO THE IRON SIGHT SECURITY DATABASE.

THE DATABASE KNOWS YOUR ONLINE HABITS, YOUR MOVEMENTS, YOUR LOCATION AND WHO YOU INTERACT WITH.

"AND, THANKS TO INFORMATION GATHERED BY YOUR PHONE CAMERAS AND ACCELEROMETERS, THE DRONES HAVE ALMOST INFALLIBLE FACIAL AND GAIT RECOGNITION."

IDENTIFIED: MASON THOMAS.

"IF YOU HAVE TOUCHED A PHONE OR TABLET, THE IRON SIGHT DRONES KNOW *EXACTLY* WHO YOU ARE."

IDENTIFIED: CLAIRE MOONEY.

TO ANY WHO WOULD HARM ANOTHER CITIZEN, THERE IS NOWHERE FOR YOU TO HIDE.

SAN FRANCISCO IS NOW A *CRIME-FREE ZONE.*

IDENTIFIED: DANIEL HALL.

STARK TOWER.

WELL.... THAT WAS TENSE.

THEY SHOULD LEAVE YOU ALONE NOW.

NOW, IF YOU'RE STAYING HERE, THERE ARE SOME HOUSE RULES.

RULE ONE. NO TOUCHING.

WHAT?

THERE ARE HUNDREDS OF FRAGILE, EXPENSIVE AND, IN SOME INSTANCES, *IRREPLACEABLE*, THINGS AROUND YOU.

YOU'RE A WALKING LUMP OF DESTRUCTION. DON'T TOUCH ANYTHING.

RULE TWO. NO MORE RAGE-FIGHTS. THAT ONE'S PRETTY SELF-EXPLANATORY.

RULE THREE. THERE WILL BE NO *"TEEN ABOMINATION"* IN THIS TOWER.

WHAT'S YOUR REAL NAME?

JAMIE.

YES.

REALLY?

NO. I CAN'T LOOK AT YOU AND SAY *"JAMIE."*

WE'LL HAVE TO WORKSHOP SOMETHING LESS INCONGRUOUS.

DID YOU MEAN WHAT YOU SAID?

ARE YOU GOING TO SAVE ME?

I'M GOING TO STUDY YOU. I'M GOING TO WORK OUT HOW YOU'VE BECOME THIS, AND I'M GOING TO LEARN FROM IT.

IF I CAN REVERSE WHAT'S HAPPENED, THEN I WILL.

WHAT ARE YOU DOING?

I THOUGHT--?

THIS ISN'T FOR YOU. YOU'RE THIRTEEN! I'M ABOUT TO HAVE COMPANY.

SPEAKING OF WHICH, MONSTERS SHOULD BE NEITHER SEEN NOR HEARD. TODDLE OFF DOWNSTAIRS.

HELLO, MATT.

HAVE YOU COME TO TAKE ME UP ON MY OFFER?

NO.

OF COURSE NOT. WHY WOULD YOU WANT YOUR SIGHT BACK? IT'S SO OVERRATED.

THE HIGH MORAL GROUND IS WAY MORE SATISFYING THAN ALL OF THE COLORS OF THE RAINBOW AND GAZING UPON THE FACES OF YOUR LOVED ONES.

SO, WHAT DO YOU WANT?

JUSTICE.

THAT'S PRETTY BROAD.

I HEARD IT.

HEARD *WHAT*?

THE TRIGGER.

I KNOW WHAT YOU'VE DONE, TONY.

EXTREMIS IS A VIRUS.

YOU CAN'T PASS A VIRUS TO A PERSON FROM A PHONE.

THE APP IS A LIE.

CAREFUL.

IT'S JUST AN INAUDIBLE DIGITAL TRIGGER-- INAUDIBLE TO EVERYONE BUT ME.

IT ACTIVATES A VIRUS THAT'S ALREADY PRESENT.

YOU'RE MAKING PEOPLE PAY FOR WHAT YOU'VE ALREADY PUT INSIDE THEM.

REALLY? HOW HAVE I DONE THAT? YOU'RE A LAWYER, MATT. DO YOU HAVE ANY PROOF OR JUST WILD THEORIES?

I KNOW WHERE TO FIND THE PROOF. I WORKED IT OUT. IT'S WHY YOU'RE IN SAN FRANCISCO.

SAN FRANCISCO BANNED THE SALE OF BOTTLED WATER.

YOU'VE PUT YOUR VIRUS IN THE WATER SUPPLY.

CLNK

SO NOW WHAT, MATT?

NOW, I LET THE F.D.A. KNOW THAT YOU'VE PUT AN UNTESTED VIRUS IN A CITY'S WATER SUPPLY. I REPRESENT THEM AGAINST YOU. AND YOU GO TO JAIL FOR A *VERY LONG TIME*.

NO!

YOU CAN'T TAKE HIM AWAY! I NEED HIM!

WHAT THE--?

CRACK

GET OFF!

HNNGH!

THD

CRSSSHHH

NO!

"--THIS NEVER HAPPENED."

HE'S COMING AROUND, MISTER STARK.

MATT? MATT, CAN YOU HEAR ME?

TONY...? IS THAT YOU?

YEAH, IT'S ME. HOW ARE YOU FEELING?

I...

WHAT HAPPENED?

YOU DON'T REMEMBER?

I... I DON'T REMEMBER ANYTHING.

YOU GAVE US A BIT OF A SCARE. WE WERE FIGHTING A MONSTER. YOU TOOK A NASTY HIT.

WHAT MONSTER? DID IT...?

HE LIVES AT MY PLACE NOW. IT'S A LONG STORY. WE'LL TALK ABOUT IT LATER.

HOW LONG HAVE I BEEN OUT?

A FEW DAYS. KIRSTEN'S BARELY LEFT YOUR--

MATT!

ARE YOU ALL RIGHT?

I THINK SO. I'M JUST A BIT SCRAMBLED.

I'LL LEAVE YOU TO IT.

THE SPECIALISTS TELL ME THAT, WITH A BRAIN INJURY LIKE THIS, YOU'LL NEED TO BE CLOSELY MONITORED AND SPEND AT LEAST A FEW WEEKS IN HERE. NO OUTSIDE STIMULI AT ALL.

BUT DON'T WORRY, MATT. IT'S ALL ON ME. ALL EXPENSES WILL BE COVERED AND I WILL HAVE MY VERY BEST PEOPLE LOOKING AFTER YOU.

YOU'RE IN *SAFE HANDS.*

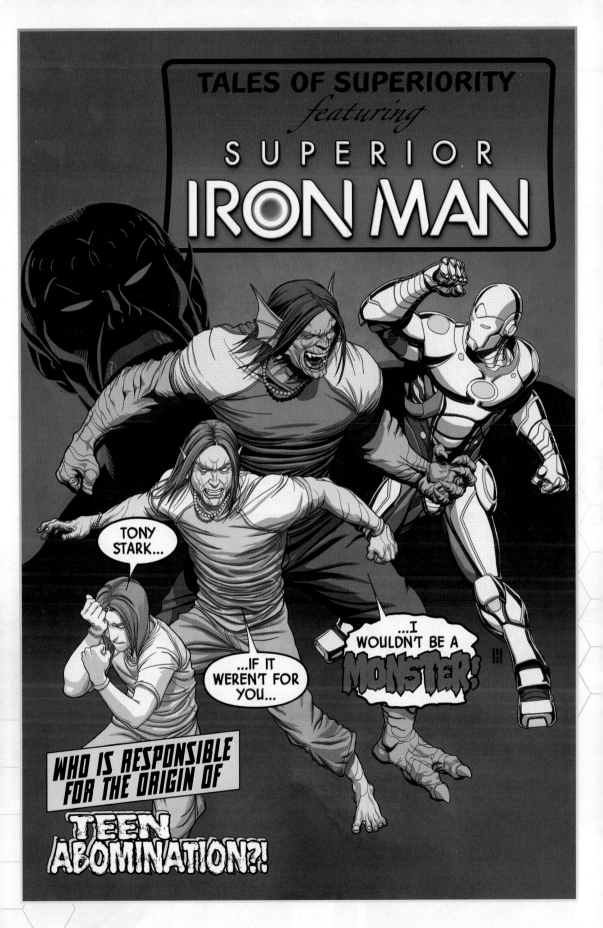

5: THE ORIGIN OF TEEN ABOMINATION

STARK ISLAND.

I'M NOT GOING TO LIE--

--THIS COULD *STING A BIT.*

WHY DO YOU HAVE TO TIE MY ARMS DOWN?

LAST TIME YOU GOT ANGRY, YOU THREW A SUPER HERO THROUGH A WINDOW.

I'D LIKE TO TAKE A SMALL BLOOD SAMPLE WITHOUT THE RISK OF DEFENESTRATION.

SO ALL THIS IS TO TAKE SOME BLOOD?

YOU HAVE ALMOST IMPENETRABLE SKIN.

BUT IF I'M BEING HONEST, NONE OF THAT IS TO TAKE BLOOD. IT'S ALL JUST A *DISTRACTION.*

HUH...?

AAAAGHH--

NO!

PSSSH

MOM!

DEET

DECEMBER THIRTEENTH, EIGHT YEARS AGO.

IT WAS SUPPOSED TO BE A GIANT LEAP FORWARD FOR CANCER TREATMENT.

IF IT WORKED, IT WOULD HAVE MADE THE GAMMA KNIFE* LOOK LIKE A BLUNT INSTRUMENT.

*THE GAMMA KNIFE IS A REAL MEDICAL TOOL AND NOT SOMETHING BRUCE BANNER INVENTED. -DOC PANIC!

TWO PEOPLE WERE CRITICALLY INJURED.

YOU REMEMBER?

I REMEMBER READING THE REPORT. SOME OF THOSE DAYS ARE A BIT... HAZY.

MY MOM SAID IT HAPPENED BECAUSE YOU WERE NEGLECTING THE COMPANY.

I WAS.

SHE WAS *FIRED.*

BY ME?

NO. SHE COULDN'T SEE YOU.

YEAH. I WAS ALWAYS BUSY BACK THEN. LEADING A DOUBLE LIFE DIDN'T LEAVE MUCH ROOM FOR THE LITTLE THINGS.

LITTLE THINGS?

AND THAT WAS THE DAY THE BLACK LAMA RETURNED.

WHAT?

"--BUT IT ALMOST KILLED ME. I BARELY MADE IT BACK TO STARK INDUSTRIES IN ONE PIECE."

KPOOOOM

TONY!

HAPPY.

GET PEPPER.

WE NEED TO... TO...

"AND THEN..."

AND THEN?

I...

I CAN'T REMEMBER.

HOW DID A LLAMA BEAT YOU?

WHAT?

I MEAN, IT HAS HOOVES. HOW DID IT HOLD THE ORB THING? WAS IT TIED AROUND ITS NECK OR...?

I WASN'T FIGHTING A--

HE WAS A POWERFUL MYSTIC!

HUH?

A *LAMA*, ONE 'L'. LIKE A GURU.

YOU WERE PICTURING ME FIGHTING AN *ACTUAL* LLAMA?

WELL... YEAH.

YOU... FORGET IT.

THE REPORT SAID TWO PEOPLE WERE BADLY INJURED IN THE EXPLOSION. IT DIDN'T MENTION THE CREATION OF A FIVE-YEAR-OLD MONSTER...?

NO.

SO WHEN DID THIS HAPPEN?

"TWO WEEKS AGO."

YOU @#$%!

HNF!

NO!

PLEASE, TROY! DON'T--

UHHF!

NO!

CRACK

WELL, YEAH. THAT'D DO IT.

THAT EXPLAINS WHY YOU HAVEN'T CHANGED BACK.

IF YOUR TRANSFORMATION IS BROUGHT ON BY ANGER...WELL, YOU'RE GOING TO BE PISSED AT YOURSELF FOREVER OVER THIS.

WHAT ABOUT YOUR DAD? WHERE'S HE IN ALL THIS?

WELL--

I DON'T KNOW. I DON'T KNOW WHO HE IS.

--YOU'RE ABOUT TO.

HUH?

I SAID THIS THING WOULD TELL US EVERYTHING. THAT INCLUDES...

Maternal mother: KATRINA CARLSON

HAPPY?

HAPPY HOGAN IS MY DAD?

WAS YOUR DAD.

HE DIED.

OKAY.

YOU'RE THE SON OF ONE OF THE FEW PEOPLE I ACTUALLY CARED ABOUT.

I *AM* GOING TO HELP YOU NOW.

YOU ALREADY SAID YOU WERE GOING TO HELP ME...?

YES. BUT IN ACTUALITY, I WAS GOING TO PULL YOU APART AND WORK OUT WHAT YOUR CELLS ARE DOING IN ORDER TO HARNESS YOUR CONDITION FOR FUN AND PROFIT.

DON'T GET ME WRONG, I'M STILL GOING TO FIND A WAY TO MONETIZE ALL OF THIS.

BUT I'LL ALSO SPEND SOME TIME TRYING TO WORK OUT HOW TO REVERSE WHAT'S HAPPENED TO YOU.

WE'LL START TOMORROW.

DO YOU NEED TO GO OUT AND PROTECT THE CITY?

NO. I'VE SET UP A HUGE NETWORK OF FLOATING CAMERAS THAT MONITOR THE ENTIRE POPULACE AND CAN SEE THROUGH WALLS.

NO ONE IN SAN FRANCISCO IS DOING ANYTHING THEY SHOULDN'T BE. THEY KNOW THEY'RE BEING WATCHED. MOST OF THEM ARE JUST THINKING UP REALLY CREATIVE WAYS NOT TO BE NAKED.

"NOW RUN OFF TO BED. THERE'S SOMETHING ELSE I NEED TO SEE TO."

ACCESS ARMOR FOOTAGE. EIGHT YEARS AGO, DECEMBER THIRTEENTH.

NO FOOTAGE FOUND. DECEMBER THIRTEENTH ARMOR VIDEO STREAM HAS BEEN DELETED.

ACCESS ALL STARK SECURITY FOOTAGE FROM DECEMBER THIRTEENTH, EIGHT YEARS AGO.

CROSS-REFERENCE WITH FACIAL RECOGNITION. DISPLAY ALL FOOTAGE CONTAINING STARK, TONY.

NO FOOTAGE FOUND. MULTIPLE FILES HAVE BEEN DELETED FROM MAIN DRIVES AND CLOUD SERVERS.

I'VE LOST TIME.

SOMEONE HAS TAKEN A DAY FROM ME.

NOW *WHO* COULD HAVE DONE SOMETHING LIKE THAT?

TO BE CONTINUED...

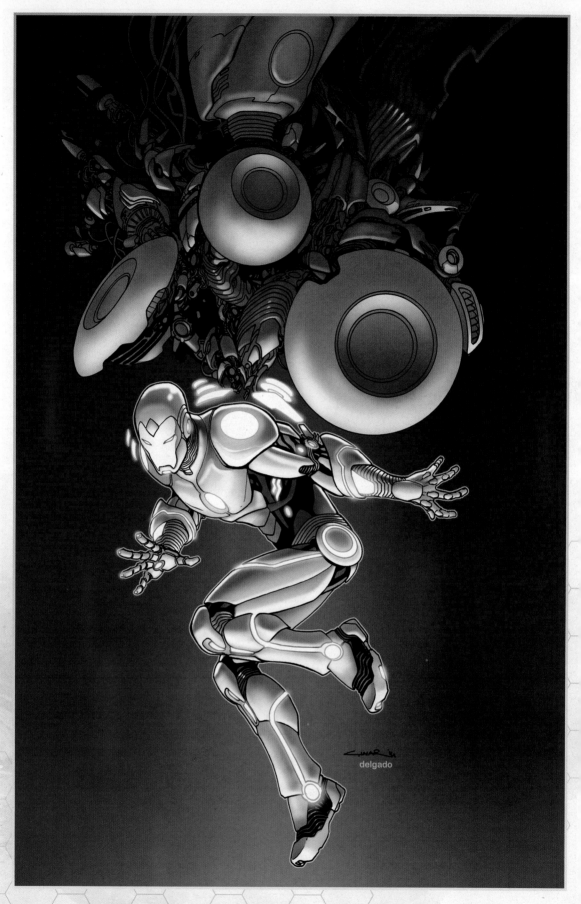

#1 DESIGN VARIANT
BY YILDIRAY ÇINAR & EDGAR DELGADO

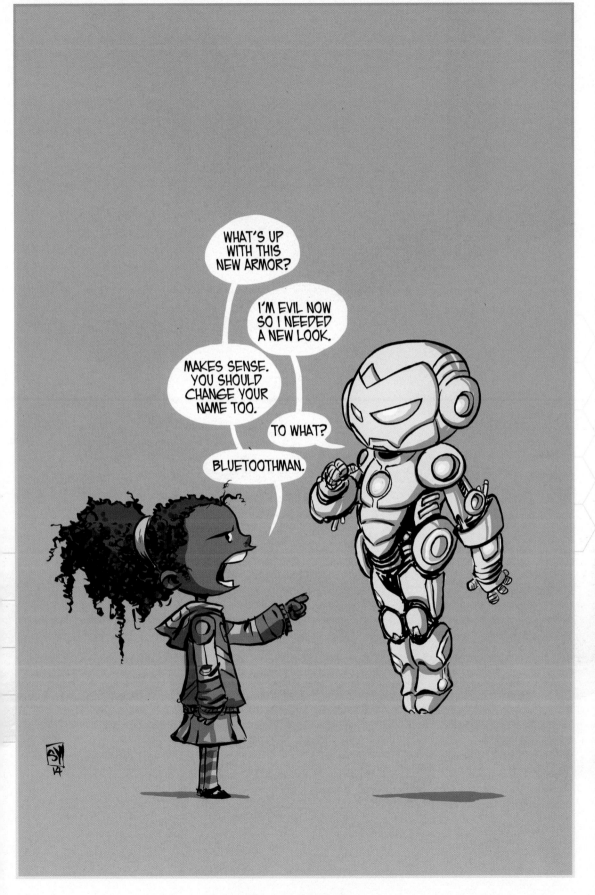

#1 VARIANT
BY SKOTTIE YOUNG

#1 VARIANT
BY MIKE PERKINS & ANDY TROY

#1 VARIANT
BY SARA PICHELLI & LAURA MARTIN

#1 75ᵀᴴ ANNIVERSARY SKETCH VARIANT
BY ALEX ROSS

#1 75TH ANNIVERSARY VARIANT
BY ALEX ROSS

#1 WIZARD VARIANT
BY TY TEMPLETON

be superior.

#3 VARIANT
BY YILDIRAY ÇINAR & JORDAN THOMAS BOYD

#4 WELCOME HOME VARIANT
BY SALVADOR LARROCA & ISRAEL SILVA

BEHIND THE IRON CURTAIN

Hey readers! Resident shell head editor Mark Paniccia here. Thought you might like a peek behind the creative process of Marvel's latest (and most unexpected) version of Tony Stark.

While Rick Remender was planning a crazy little thing that became AVENGERS AND X-MEN: AXIS, one of the ideas everyone here at MARVEL gravitated to was seeing bad guys become good guys and good guys become bad guys. With the right characters, attitudinal adjustments and creative teams, we knew some wild stories could spin out of the event…and seeing a more devious Tony Stark unleashed on the MARVEL UNIVERSE kind of gave us all goose bumps. What would happen if the golden Avenger wasn't so golden anymore? I couldn't see Tony Stark going completely evil, but I could see him go…chrome!

Let me explain. When I talked to writer Tom Taylor about the book, we thought an extreme version of a pre-heart-injury Tony Stark personality was the way to go. As a hero, we know Tony as a good looking, stylish, confident yet fair and noble guy… but without that moral compass — that perspective he gained when Ho Yinsen sacrificed himself so Tony could escape his captors — he'd feel…SUPERIOR. He would be self-indulgent, vain and over-the-top. I'd seen a picture of a chromed luxury sports car and thought that was a pretty good example of over-the-top. We wanted to lean into the narcissism, selfishness and glam of this altered Tony Stark with a super- sleek, LED, futuristic armor, and the mirror-like quality of chrome fed into that perfectly.

Artist Yildiray Çinar's first designs for SUPERIOR IRON MAN

We told artist Yildiray Çınar and he promptly started enthusiastically sketching away at designs. We wanted to have blue LED stretch throughout and Tom had the idea that they could turn red when Tony was about to attack, giving him "a bit of menace."

More early ideas from Yiliray

You wouldn't like Tony when he's angry (and glowing red)!

We asked Yildiray to add holographic elements and have the readouts and graphs surround Tony's head. I suggested Tony not even have a faceplate. Vain Tony would want everyone to see his beautiful face. When Yildiray did helmet designs, we decided to keep the option of having the faceplate, and Tom came up with the idea of using stealth graphene for protective measures. All of Yildiary's sketches were cool but we especially liked having the eyebrows hidden, making Tony look more distant and regal.

The final helmet design incorporated many elements seen in these four versions.

We ended up with a lot of great designs from Yildiray. The "Superior" armor still has a classic super hero vibe to it while messaging the stuff under the surface. Hope you dig it as much as we do.

The next thing on the sketch list was the new Stark Tower. With Tony's unchecked ego at play, what could we do that would one-up what MARVEL's most successful and famous businessman has already done? Well, during early AXIS conversations between Rick Remender and Tom Taylor, the idea of Tony setting up shop on Alcatraz came up and dang was it a brilliant idea! Besides working on several levels, it allowed us to "upgrade" Stark Tower from the standard impressive skyscraper to a much more imposing piece of real estate. Thus what we now call STARK ISLAND was born!

We asked Yildiray to come up with something that would not only be an aesthetic extension of the armor (sleek and futuristic) but a design that exuded Tony's amped up lust for spectacle. This had to be the kind of place you'd see from a million miles away, looked beautiful and screamed good times! Personally I love it. If I could have blue LED everywhere in my house I would.

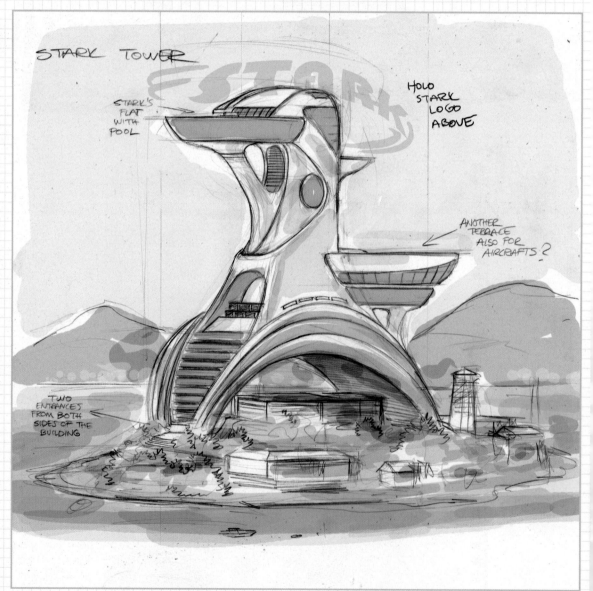

STARK TOWER

STARK'S FLAT WITH POOL

HOLO STARK LOGO ABOVE

ANOTHER TERRACE ALSO FOR AIRCRAFTS?

TWO ENTRANCES FROM BOTH SIDES OF THE BUILDING

Yildiray's concept art for Stark Island, where all the cool Extremis-modified people hang.

1.

2.

Extremis 3.0 app designs. All so good I wished there was an app to help us choose.

Another important visual element was the app design for Extremis 3.0. In-house designer Summer Lacy provided us with six different options. And we loved 'em all. Tom was especially drawn to #5, commenting that it was "all kinds of genius." It was a hard decision but after going back and forth a few times we finally settled on #2, beautifully simple yet layered in meaning. Summer was good enough to design the recap page where the app icon is a key image really helping to give the book a unique vibe.

Before I go I'd like to give a shout out to Summer Lacy who did an awesome job on the logo and recap design and Irene Y. Lee and Nelson Ribiero for their great design contributions.

Mark Paniccia
Senior Editor
MARVEL COMICS

So...TEEN ABOMINATION started as a joke.

In fact, at one stage, he wasn't even Teen Abomination. He was, ridiculously, named TEEN MAN-THING.

Some jokes stay jokes. Some jokes grow legs, grow long hair, grow green, and get their own origin in the MARVEL UNIVERSE. This joke did this because he quickly stopped being a joke and became something else.

One of the challenges with writing SUPERIOR IRON MAN is that our main character is... well, kind of a *jerk*. You're not supposed to like him. Sure, you can enjoy his antics and his humor and his ego but this isn't the Tony we all know and love anymore. He's pretty unlikeable.

But stories need characters readers can root for. This was one of the reasons MATT MURDOCK was chosen to stand against Tony in our first arc. Matt is a guy we all root for, and seeing this twisted Tony from Matt's perspective really helped us shape our SUPERIOR IRON MAN.

While Teen Abomination was originally created pretty much just for Tony to poke fun at and dismiss, our whole team, and especially Editor Mark Paniccia, really liked him. We all felt sorry for him as soon as we saw his humanity through Yildiray's art.

I remember Mark actually asked me to make sure Teen Abomination didn't really hurt anyone. He really liked the character and wanted him to be redeemable. Mark became really protective of Teen Abomination. So much so, he was even protecting him from me.

And so, when Mark asked me to write a flashback issue for Laura Braga in issue #5, I knew what I wanted to do. I wanted to tell the tragic origin of Teen Abomination. A young kid, bullied at school for being outside the mainstream, who was already feeling a bit uncomfortable in his own skin, who becomes trapped in far worse skin.

The challenge was then to tie him to our story and our characters in a fundamental way - to tie him to Tony. And I wanted even the cold, calculating heart of Superior Tony Stark to see what we saw in Teen Abomination. I wanted to give Superior Tony Stark someone he would feel protective of. We hope you'll feel protective of him too.

Tom Taylor

First version of Teen Abomination by Yildiray Çınar.

Take two leaning more towards a Hulk vibe.

Teen Abomination from issue #4, page 14